To Andrea, the refiner of my dreams

and for Ken Tyler
who is still learning his ABCs

Special thanks to James Sewell
for some coloration and lots of erasing
(and also the endsheet design)

THE GREAT ALPHABET FIGHT
published by Gold'n'Honey Books
Questar Publishers, Inc.

Illustrations: © 1993 by Joni Eareckson Tada
Text: © 1993 by Steve Jensen

International Standard Number: 0-88070-612-0

Printed in the United States of America

For information:
Questar Publishers, Inc.
Post Office Box 1720
Sisters, Oregon 97759

93 94 95 96 97 98 99 00 01 — 10 9 8 7 6 5 4 3 2 1

The Great ALPHABET FIGHT

STORY BY STEVE JENSEN

ILLUSTRATIONS BY JONI EARECKSON TADA

Gold 'n' Honey BOOKS

In that lazy time between reading and recess, I closed my eyes to find…

…a secret door.

With a dream and a glance I crawled into…

a room that smelled like my grandfather's attic. The walls were covered with paper that was bumpy and peeling. The floor creaked as I stepped on its boards. Books lay everywhere — on the shelves and on the floor.

"Where am I?" I wondered. "This place looks so old…it can't be my school."

Sunlight shown ahead and I followed on tiptoes.

"It's so quiet; I wonder if I should be here. I wasn't invited, and I should really go back to school…"

But I couldn't resist just one step more.

HISTORY
of the
ALPHABET
COUNCIL
by
J. Butler

What a surprise! I *was* in school after all! It wasn't my school of metal and noise, but an old school of wood and quiet. The room was empty except for one hamster and a turtle in a fish bowl. The drips of soggy mittens splashed and sizzled on the fat, round stove.

I walked to the front and stopped beside the teacher's desk.

"Where is everyone?" I wondered aloud. "What kind of school has no teachers or kids?"

"A school where words are born, of course!" came a reply.

I turned toward the voice
but saw no one there.
Only a row of letters
pinned to the board.

"Who said that?" I asked.

"Who else but me!" said the letter T. "And I'm tough enough to teach you some lessons, you know!"

Two letters popped off and danced a duet.

"If you sneeze," said G, "I'll say, 'God bless you.'"
"And if you wipe your nose on your sleeve," said Mrs. M,
"I'll say, 'Mind your manners, young man!'"

"Welcome to our school," greeted A. "I'm afraid you've come
at a most embarrassing time."

"The letters C and E are in the midst of a fight. They live next door to each other in the alphabet, you see, and—well, we've been trying to find a way to make them stop. But it's no use. We've given up."

Before A could explain, I heard an angry cry…

"I don't like you, letter E," said C. "And I don't like your silly words—especially eggplant and elephant!"

"Oh, just admit it, C," said E proudly. "You wish you had my good looks. I'd be angry too if I spelled words like cranky, cold, and crabby. You ought to be easy and breezy like me!"

C began bending at the curves. "I'd never be a square-headed, three-toed egghead like you!"

C's friends tried to show him how special he was.

"Take a look, C. You're part of a great word called Excellent. It's quite an honor, don't you think?"

C's anger turned to tears, and he sniffled, "There, don't you see! E has all the luck. Look at how many E's are in Excellent!"

C crawled away to his own little world.

"Now C," said B. "You can behave better than that. Look at J. He's not in many words, but he's a jolly joker all the time.

"And look at X. She's used even less often, but she's always exciting and expressive. Never, ever cross."

"Oh, buzz off," answered C. "Nothing will ever bring E and me together again!"

The alphabet seemed doomed to have two letters at war.

"Not so fast," interrupted D. "I've been listening to all of this from my place at the end of the alphabet and I have an idea."

C and E listened but stayed far apart.

"It seems you two need a friend to bring you together. I'd be willing to give up my special place next to Z. It's worth the move to end all this fighting."

"I'd promise to share my time with both of you. When my letter is small I can chit-chat with C. And when I'm a capital, I'd be great company for E."

The other letters were excited about the idea.

"Come on, D," said A. "Quick! Move in before we lose any words over this fight."

D said goodbye to Z and made a new home between C and E.

It did not take long for things to change. D had good, long talks with his new neighbors. D showed E the fun side of C. And C saw the wonder of E. They both apologized for the way they acted.

"I'm sorry," said C, "for being so angry."

"I'm sorry for being so proud," said E.

Soon they both enjoyed being together again in words like Echo and Ice Cream.

And D became a hero. For his efforts, he was awarded new words. (Such is the custom, you know, among the letters of the alphabet.) D's new words were drawn on the board:

Everyone oohed and aahed. But there was one more word yet to be born.

A announced in a loud voice, "As a sign that the fighting between C and E is now over, we hereby declare that every quarrel should end in a new word: *peace*. It's an end to all fighting and a beginning for friends. And how perfect that every peace should end with C and E!"

"Hooray for a perfect word!" everyone shouted.
"Hooray for Peace!"

D smiled and said, "It's time you went back to class, young man.
And be sure to tell them what you've learned.
Make peace whenever you can."

"I will," I said, and I waved my dream goodbye.

Meet this book's artist —
Joni Eareckson Tada

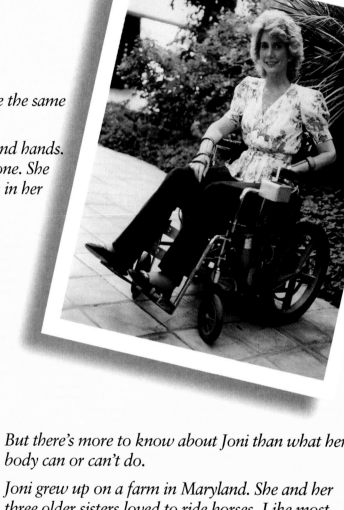

"I love hugging kids," says Joni. "They're the same height as I am in my wheelchair!"

Joni is disabled. She can't move her legs and hands. She can't feel anything below her collarbone. She can move her arms only by using muscles in her shoulder.

But there's more to know about Joni than what her body can or can't do.

Joni grew up on a farm in Maryland. She and her three older sisters loved to ride horses. Like most kids, they got into their share of fights — especially in the hay loft! Their mom and dad helped them to make peace with one another.

If she wasn't riding horses, Joni was drawing them. She drew this picture when she was six years old, waiting for her lunch at a restaurant.

Joni didn't lose her talent when she became disabled. An artist's talent is not in her hands, but in her heart.

Joni became disabled when she dove into some water and hit her head. It broke a bone in her neck. She almost drowned, but she was saved just in time.

It was very hard on Joni to not be able to move. She became an angry person (like the letter C in this story.) She felt like giving up.

But there were good friends who visited Joni and helped her understand how happy her life could be. Her anger went away.

Now Joni understood what peace really is. She could enjoy life again.

Later she met Ken Tada, and soon she married him. Ken teaches at a high school. He loves to play racquetball, and to fish in the ocean. Joni and Ken enjoy camping in the Sierra Mountains of California.

Joni's van has special equipment that lets her drive with one arm in a joystick. When she's not driving to work or church, she's enjoying butter-almond ice cream, books, music, and her dog Scruffy.

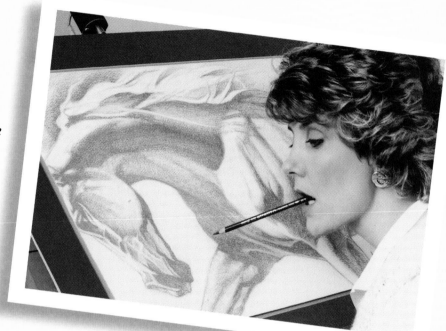

Even though she's disabled, Joni can do many things. She writes books, sings, talks to groups of people, and helps others who are disabled. And — as you can see from this book — she's also an artist.

Joni uses her mouth to draw and paint. It took her many years of practice to control the pencils and brushes. Try writing your name with your mouth sometime!

Sometimes as she draws and paints, Joni needs help from the hands of a friend — like me! We can put pencils in her mouth, or move papers around for her.

Has anyone ever told you not to chew on pencils? Well, Joni can't help it. After a day of drawing, her pencils look like they've been to an alligator zoo!

Joni travels all over the world and meets lots of people. She loves to talk with them about having peace in their hearts. Like you, she would love to see everyone live in peace. Countries wouldn't be at war, and families and friends would get along.

Making peace isn't always easy. It takes courage to say you're sorry, or to help someone stop fighting. But we need people just like you who are willing to do that!